THIS BOOK BELONGS TO:

Test Your Colors Here

Test Your Colors Here

Scan me!
FOR MORE PRODUCT

azbookland.com

THANK YOU FOR BEING
OUR VALUED CUSTOMER
WE WOULD BE GRATEFUL

Made in the USA
Coppell, TX
05 November 2024

39709814R00037